THE KNACK OF MEDITATION

The No-Nonsense Guide to Successful Meditation

by
Paul Mason

PREMANAND
premanandpaul@yahoo.co.uk
www.paulmason.info

© Paul Mason 2013
First published by Premanand 2013
revision 2015, 2020
ISBN 978-0-9562228-3-1

Cover, design & typesetting by Premanand

Foreword

Let me share a tale with you …

"It was a snap decision to buy the old wooden armchair from the secondhand furniture shop. I was seventeen years old, had the money spare, and on an impulse suddenly decided I wanted to buy it for myself. I had never bought an item of furniture before and I enjoyed the freedom of making a choice over what I sat on at home – I placed it in my bedroom in a corner near the window. It didn't cost a lot so I didn't get to regretting it. I was working at that time, and recall that when I came home I would, more often than not, park myself down on my armchair, get comfortable and close my eyes for a while. It was my bit of lazy time. I would sit just watching my thoughts until there appeared to be no thoughts to watch. Then, I would open my eyes and look around at my bedroom and enjoy just being me and having all my stuff around me.

As it happened, my routine would soon become disrupted. I left that job, and I lost the habit of sitting in the chair too.

I would not describe myself as a contemplative person, nor would I say I am particularly patient, so I am not the sort of person that one would necessarily associate with being interested in meditation, in fact, at that time, I wasn't really, other than having a mild curiousity about it. However, that was to change!

I first realised I needed to meditate when I felt an internal pressure, an unrest, an unfamiliar and intense discomfort, which I wanted to dissolve or remove myself from. But, though I experimented unsuccessfully at gazing at a candle I realised I just wasn't 'getting it', actually, it was making matters worse, making me feel much worse!

Some months later, whilst travelling with my girlfriend, I was given a pep talk on meditation, and I was persuaded to learn how to meditate, which occurred the very next day. The technique involved the repetition of a *mantra*, a special word which was meaningless to me, and the general idea was that I should not sit there thinking my thoughts but to instead repeat the *mantra* until arriving at the source of thought, to a state of tranquil awareness. Well it sounded good but in truth the 'blissful restful alertness' did not happen for me. So, rather naughtily, and I decided to give up repeating the *mantra* and let go of thoughts - just to see what would happen. Well, the first thing that 'happened' is that I heard clearly the sounds in the garden outside, and then, well…..the extraoridinary truth is that it happened just the way I had been told. I found myself in a state of tranquil awareness. - I was delighted, utterly delighted.

The effects of that experience lingered with me, so I decided to keep the practice of meditation going, but forgot the little trick of not using the *mantra* and just letting go, and it became more difficult to access that state of tranquility, which was a shame, because though meditation became a routine for me, it did not always give me the peace of mind I craved. But I consoled myself that one day it would all resolve and my meditations would get better, and sometimes they did, but I still did not find tranquility on tap.

Something happened to make me question again the practice of meditation. I happened to be in India, where I had been for a couple of weeks or so, and had sat down to meditate but somehow, on this occasion, I could not think the *mantra*, I just couldn't do it, try as I might to recall and repeat it, it just would not happen, so instead, I just sat and enjoyed doing nothing instead. The experience was just astonishing, time kind of stopped still, I found myself bathed in tranquility – deep, deep satisfaction was here at hand.

I visited someone I had met a few days earlier, a rather wonderful soul called Dandi Swami Narayananand Saraswati – and took along some fruit and a few of sprigs of *Bourganvillia* and red *Rhodedendron* flowers.

After several minutes walk into the jungle I neared the place the *swami* stayed. As I waited around for him I made conversation with a TM teacher friend who casually described him, "Oh yes, he is enlightened, he is *guru*!"

When Swami Narayananand and I were alone he approved my teaching meditation.

Well, after such an intense experience with my meditation you might imagine that I would completely abandon TM and just adopt a routine of sitting with my eyes closed and settling down naturally. No, I continued with my regular practice.

But the experience left me intensely curious. I wanted to find out more about the variety of ways that people meditate and which ways seem to work best and why.

I looked into the topic of meditation deeply, and in so doing discovered many varied descriptions of how the practice of meditation is best done..

I was really surprised and pleased to discover how many prominent teachers seem agree on the basics, so I have collected together some of their descriptions in order for others to see, along with a simplified guide on how meditation can be practiced successfully."

Acknowledgements

The author is grateful to those publications tand websites hat have furnished the quotations included in this volume, which have then been used on the terms of 'fair useage'

Illustrations

All images used are believed to be in the public domain. Photos have been substantially enhanced by digital editing techniques in order to present them more clearly, and, as such, are unique images.

Should anyone raise a valid objection against any image being included, the publisher would consider substituting another image in its place.

Contents

THE KNACK OF MEDITATION

INTRODUCTION

Meditation is certainly not a modern idea as forms of meditation have been with us for thousands of years!

Thought-free meditation is detailed in ancient writings and has been advocated widely over many centuries

Unfortunately, information concerning thought-free meditation is scarce today and, where it is available, the practice is seldom described clearly, or instruction offered freely.

All-too-often talk about meditation is confused and confusing.

If those learning to meditate hear suggestions such as 'go deep', 'go beyond thought', 'empty the mind', 'blank the mind', they can easily become confused and get put off. Such instructions are quite misleading and make it all-too-easy for people to imagine that meditation involves discomfort or dissociation. Indeed, the topic of meditation is so muddled that some even fear they might fall prey to self-hypnosis or find themselves in a trance!?!

Here, in this book, thought-free meditation is explained, clearly and simply. Guidance is offered independent of any personality, *guru*, cult, or belief system.

WHAT IS MEDITATION?

Meditation is an age-old practice described in ancient texts of various cultures across the world, some more than 2000 years ago.

Meditation is variously referred to as *'Dhyana'* in Sanskrit, *'Ch'an'* in Chinese, *'Zen'* in Japanese, and *'Sgom'* in Tibetan.

Thought-free meditation is sometimes referred to as the 'Royal Path' or 'Raja Yoga' (*'râjâ'* = king i.e. royal).

Authentic thought-free meditation can be practiced by anyone regardless of beliefs, or lack of beliefs.

Meditation is a very useful practice.

WHY MEDITATE?

There are various reasons why people are drawn to the practice of meditation – for instance, the desire to simplify, to neutralize stress and to come to terms with oneself, and the wish to relax, to find inner happiness and experience stillness and tranquility.

We live in an age where it is increasingly difficult to keep up with pace of change, where we are overloaded with images, sounds and ideas from multiple sources. So, it essential we find sufficient peace of mind in order to live such a lifestyle - meditation fulfils this need.

Meditation is a gift to ourselves as no fee is payable for understanding or practicing meditation.

Meditation is completely natural.

WHEN TO MEDITATE?

Soon!

There are no hard and fast rules about when to meditate - but best not to practice if you are too tired, or have just eaten a meal, or are in an induced state of consciousness (through drink or drugs).

24

HOW TO MEDITATE?

The Practice of Meditation Explained in 7 Easy Stages

Meditation – 1st Stage

Find somewhere comfortable enough for you to sit, where you are unlikely to be interrupted for at least half an hour or for as long as you wish to meditate. If you choose to sit in the traditional crossed-legged pose, sit with a thick cushion beneath the bottom, to prevent strain to the knees and spine. It cannot be stressed too much that when you sit to meditate you should be comfortable!

Meditation – 2nd Stage

Settle for a short while, and then close the eyes.

Closing the eyes, perhaps you feel some stillness, some quietness, some silence?

No doubt thoughts will arise whilst you sit.

Thinking is a natural process.

Thinking occurs without effort.

Enjoy the thoughts.

Meditation – 3rd Stage

Then place your attention on something other than thoughts. This can easily be achieved by placing one's attention onto airborne sounds or on to one's own breath. Or one can direct the attention to the sensation of light within, which at first might appear very faint but can become quite intense on occasion.

Meditation - 4th Stage

Gradually, gradually minimise and decrease mental activity, but do this reasonably gently. The mind seems to be active just because that is its habit. See the thoughts as just the apparently endless workings of your mind, which ought to be allowed to take a break.

It is time to exercise one's mental brakes, very lightly but firmly.

See the thoughts for what they are - just mental activity - and realise that this would be a good time for the mind to be less active.

If the mind is determined to go on being active redirect it to awareness of the breath or just listen to outer sounds, just place your attention on the sounds without involvement.

Do not resist sounds you may hear whilst meditating, just listen and accept (respond to sounds only if there is some good reason).

If you get caught up in a whole load of thinking, that's fine, just observe the thoughts. Agitating against thoughts is counter-productive, so just relax.

Don't be unduly frustrated if you do not readily sustain a state of no thought. Just be a witness to the experience, this is meditation.

Whilst you are sitting quietly witnessing the thoughts that come and go, the body may, from time to time, draw your attention. Both the mind and body are settling down.

Meditation - 5th Stage

Ask yourself what it would be like to sit without thoughts.

Remind yourself that you are giving your mind permission to quieten and be without thoughts for a while. The mind might rebel against this idea. No problem, don't force the issue. But from time-to-time summon this idea again. At some time the mind will be curious enough to co-operate.

Meditation - 6th Stage

The meditative state is found to be a state of alert passivity, and is often accompanied by reduced breathing.

When the state of no-thought is arrived at there is nothing to do!

This state of no-thought is a chance for the mind and body to relax for a while. Indeed, whilst in this state of mind there can be no anxieties, no concerns about what is past, no worries about the present or the future. It is a truly refreshing experience.

Meditation - 7th Stage

When you feel the wish to resume activity again then gently open the eyes and slowly re-adjust to your surroundings before getting up.

HOW WAS YOUR MEDITATION?

Hopefully, you relaxed and didn't put any effort into 'trying' to meditate - it is important to be without expectations in meditation and not to force anything, else you might find yourself with a headache!

Take it easy and don't get achievement-orientated - just relax, and, when a moment comes to let go, then let go of the thoughts and enjoy the natural result.

Remember, don't get frustrated trying to achieve anything in your meditation. Just find time to sit again and again to meditate.

Meditation is well described as a 'circuit breaker'.

If you find yourself falling asleep during meditation, don't resist (unless you have some prior appointment or duty).

If you have fallen asleep during your meditation, then, once you have awoken sufficiently, open the eyes and re-engage with everyday activity.

TOO WOUND UP TO MEDITATE?

It is possible that some may feel unable or unready to practice meditation, on account of being unable to relax long enough, unable to sit and close their eyes for more than a couple of minutes or so.

Some people are convinced that they are too wound up to meditate but believe that certain techniques, such as using an additive such as a *mantra* to distract and please the mind, or dwelling on certain thoughts, or contemplating certain qualities such as love and compassion, can help them settle down.

Indeed, if you have already been taught a meditation technique that you value, you can practice that technique until you settle down somewhat, and then follow the tips about letting go of thoughts.

Certainly, if one chooses to use a *mantra* given by a meditation teacher, then the advice is just not to 'hold on' to the *mantra,* if it slips away just sit for a while neither thinking the *mantra* nor thinking thought!

So, just go with your own choice of 'technique', if you use one, and when the mind has settled somewhat, and the thought comes to let go of thought, then simply go with that.

As long as you are settling down and are not straining to achieve something, the mind will find that moment to let go of the mind-chatter and be free to just indwell.

It is about choice, your choice, nobody is pressurising you.

BENEFITS OF REGULAR MEDITATION

It has been pointed out that this process of clearing the mind of thoughts is useful in preparing to go to sleep. It would be great if it were also adopted as a means of waking up!

It is not uncommon for practitioners of meditation to sit for two periods per day, once in the morning and once in the evening. If in doubt as to how long to sit for meditation, a widely used method is to sit for the length of time a medium length stick of incense takes to burn down, say about twenty minutes or half an hour, whatever suits you. However, it is not necessarily beneficial to meditate for particularly long periods or to meditate more frequently. Ideally, one should live a balanced life, so meditate for a while and then get up and get on with the everyday life.

It is held that the experience of meditation is

extremely beneficial, both physically and mentally. as apparently experience of the thought-free wakeful state gives rise to positive changes of brain chemistry (allegedly linked to an increase in levels of dopamine). It is also taught that the repeated conscious experience of the state of no-thought (sometimes referred to as Pure Consciousness) eventually gives rise to a permanent state of higher awareness. Pure consciousness is a level of consciousness that underlies the three basic states of consciousness, viz. waking, dreaming and deep sleep. In Sanskrit this pure consciousness is called *'turiya'*, *'chaturya'* or *'chaturtha'* meaning fourth. The repeated experience of this Pure Consciousness can be likened to oil being poured, flowing into the other three states of consciousness, oiling the mechanisms of perception, thereby bringing greater freshness, clarity, and purpose to everyday life.

In many traditions and cultures it is taught that such prolonged experience of Pure Consciousness is the basis of 'enlightenment' (definition and description of this exalted state varies). All told, the experience of thought-free meditation is held to be extremely positive with enjoyment of the now being its chief purpose.

ARE ALL MEDITATION METHODS EQUALLY USEFUL?

Nowadays a very wide variety of meditation methods are available, though not all meditators are guided to a thought-free state.

Meditative techniques that engage the mind or imagination seem popular, especially those taught in groups, which rely on visualization or focus on qualities of sensation, colour or sound. Though these teachings may initially appear attractive, they are unlikely to do more than affect a temporary change to mood levels, without producing significant long-term benefits.

Also popular are those less accessible esoteric teachings, often purporting to be from a special lineage or an ancient tradition, revealing secret practices only to committed 'initiates'. Though it is tempting to believe that such-and-such a teaching can miraculously transform one's life - be aware - initiates can find themselves disappointed, disillusioned, ill-used and impoverished. Beware of cults!

The important thing to realise about meditation is that, unless a 'thought-free state' is attained, one is still involved in the incessant activity of the mind, regardless of how interesting that might be.

So, at some time, you need to give yourself a break from the seemingly endless process of thinking, thinking, thinking, thinking ....

Question: ***'Why don't more meditators reach the "thought-free" state?'***

Gary Weber (author of 'Happiness Beyond Thought'): ***'One of the most important limitations is not knowing that a state of "no thoughts" is possible, desirable, or useful. Having few thoughts is not something described cryptically in obscure texts of one small sect. The state of "no thoughts" has been described by many leading spiritual figures in many different traditions.'***

http://happinessbeyondthought.blogspot.co.uk

Contained in the Scriptures of various cultures are numerous references to the practice of thought-free meditation, and over the centuries many thinkers, spiritual teachers and *gurus* have emphasised the importance and value of this practice. This fact seems to have escaped most people's notice, resulting in many getting caught up with strange beliefs, imaginings and the occult. Interestingly, the wave of 20th Century teachers, though critical of one another's teachings, appears to have been united in praise of thought-free meditation! But, rather than publicise their views on thought-free meditation, these controversial figures instead spread their own philosophies and practices.

THE KNACK OF MEDITATION

42

A Selection of Quotations relating to Thought-Free Meditation
- ancient, modern & contemporary - Indian, Chinese, Japanese, Christian & others

- Important -
No endorsement of any individual or organization quoted
is implied or intended.

Bhairava - Shiva – Shankar
Mahadeva -Yogiraj

Dharana (Attention) on Thought-Free-Ness

यत्र यत्र मनो याति तत्तत्तेनैव तत्क्षणम् ।

परित्यज्यानवस्थित्या निस्तरङ्गस्ततो भवेत् ॥

yatra yatra mano yāti tattattenaiva tatkṣaṇam |

parityajyānavasthityā nistaraṅgastato bhavet ||

'The very moment that the mind goes wandering, that inattentiveness is to be abandoned - stillness should follow.'

Vigyana Bhairava Tantra, verse 129

Lord Krishna in meditation

Bhagavad Gita – 'Lord's Song'
c.5th Century BC

शुचौ देशे प्रतिष्ठाप्य स्थिरमासनमात्मनः ।

नात्युच्छ्रितं नातिनीचं चैलाजिनकुशोत्तरम् ॥ ११ ॥

तत्रैकाग्रं मनः कृत्वा यतचित्तेन्द्रियक्रियाः ।

उपविश्यासने युञ्ज्याद्योगमात्मविशुद्धये ॥ १२ ॥

समं कायशिरोग्रीवं धारयन्नचलं स्थिरः ।

संप्रेक्ष्य नासिकाग्रं स्वं दिशश्चानवलोकयन् ॥ १३ ॥

सङ्कल्पप्रभवान्कामांस्त्यक्त्वा सर्वानशेषतः ।

मनसैवेन्द्रियग्रामं विनियम्य समन्ततः ॥ २४ ॥

शनैः शनैरुपरमेद् बुद्ध्या धृतिगृहीतया ।

आत्मसंस्थं मनः कृत्वा न किंचिदपि चिन्तयेत् ॥ २५ ॥

यतो यतो निश्चरति मनश्चंचलमस्थिरम् ।

ततस्ततो नियम्यैतदात्मन्येव वशं नयेत् ॥ २६ ॥

प्रशान्तमनसं ह्येनं योगिनं सुखमुत्तमम् ।

उपैति शान्तरजसं ब्रह्मभूतमकल्मषम् ॥ २७ ॥

śucau deśe pratiṣṭhāpya sthiramāsanamātmanaḥ |

nātyucchritaṁ nātinīcaṁ cailājinakuśottaram || 6:11||

tatraikāgraṁ manaḥ kṛtvā yatacittendriyakriyāḥ |

upaviśyāsane yuñjyādyogamātmaviśuddhaye || 6:12||

samaṁ kāyaśirogrīvaṁ dhārayannacalaṁ sthiraḥ |

samprekśya nāsikāgraṁ svaṁ diśaścānavalokayan || 6:13||

saṅkalpaprabhavānkāmāṁstyaktvā sarvānaśeṣataḥ |

manasaivendriyagrāmaṁ viniyamya samantataḥ || 6:24||

śanaiḥ śanairuparamed buddhyā dhṛtigṛhītayā |

ātmasaṁsthaṁ manaḥ kṛtvā na kiñcidapi cintayet || 6:25||

yato yato niścarati manaścañcalamasthiram |

tatastato niyamyaitadātmanyeva vaśaṁ nayet || 6:26||

praśāntamanasaṁ hyenaṁ yoginaṁ sukhamuttamam |

upaiti śāntarajasaṁ brahmabhūtamakalmaṣam || 6:27||

'In a clean spot, having set a firm seat (cushion) of his own, neither too high nor too low, made of cloth, a deerskin and kusha-grass, one upon the other. Gita 6:11

'There, having made the mind one-pointed, with the activities of the mind and the senses controlled, let him seated on the seat, practice "yoga" for self-purification. Gita 6:12

'Let him steadily hold his body, keeping head and neck erect and still, directing the gaze towards the tip of the nose, without looking in any direction. Gita 6:13

'Abandoning without reserve all desires born of thought and imagination, and completely restraining the whole group of senses by the mind from all sides. Gita 6:24

'Gradually, gradually let him attain to quietude by firmly holding the intellect; establishing the mind in the Self; let him not think even of anything. Gita 6:25

'From whatever cause the restless and unsteady mind wanders away, from that let him restrain it and bring it under the control of the Self alone. Gita 6:26

'For supreme happiness comes to the yogi whose mind is quite peaceful, whose passion is quieted...' Gita 6:27

यदा पञ्चावतिष्ठन्ते ज्ञानानि मनसा सह ।

बुद्धिश्च न विचेष्टते तामाहुः परमां गतिम् ॥ १० ॥

तां योगमिति मन्यन्ते स्थिरामिन्द्रियधारणाम् ।

अप्रमत्तस्तदा भवति योगो हि प्रभवाप्ययौ ॥ ११ ॥

yadā pañcāvatiṣṭhante jñānāni manasā saha |
buddhiśca na viceṣṭate tāmāhuḥ paramāṁ gatim || 10||

tāṁ yogamiti manyante sthirāmindriyadhāraṇām |
apramattastadā bhavati yogo hi prabhavāpyayau || 11||

*'When the five senses are settled
and the mind has ceased to think
and the intellect does not stir
That is the highest state, they say.'*

Katha Upanishad 2-III-10 / 6.10

*'Thus "yoga" is considered to be
holding still the senses.
Then one should be alert,
for "yoga" comes and goes.'*

Katha Upanishad 2-III-11 / 6.11

Katha Upanishad
c.5th Century BC

अथ योगानुशासनम्॥ १ ॥

योगश्चित्तवृत्तिनिरोधः॥ २ ॥

तदा द्रष्टुः स्वरूपेऽवस्थानम्॥ ३ ॥

वृत्तिसारूप्यम् इतरत्र ॥ ४ ॥

atha yogānuśāsanam || 1 ||
yogaścittavṛttinirodhaḥ || 2 ||
tadā draṣṭuḥ svarūpe'vasthānam || 3 ||
vṛttisārūpyam itaratra || 4 ||

योगश्चित्तवृत्तिनिरोधः

"*Yoga* is the halting of mental activity"
(Earliest known definition of word *'yoga'* - c.3rd Century BC)

'Now, the teaching of "yoga"... 1:1

"Yoga" is "nirodha" (restraint, stopping, halting) of the "vritti" (whirling, thought-waves, mental activity) of the "chitta" (consciousness, memory, subconscious). 1:2

Then the seer rests in his own self. 1:3

At other times he is identified with the whirling [of the mind].' 1:4

Yogadarshanam - Patanjali's Yoga Sutras
c.3rd Century BC

Buddha

Dhyāna [Meditation] in Buddhism

The *jhānas* are states of meditation where the mind is free from the five hindrances - craving, aversion, sloth, agitation and doubt - and (from the second *jhāna* onwards) incapable of discursive thinking.

The Buddha also rediscovered an attainment beyond the dimension of neither perception nor non-perception, Nirodha-Samapatti, the "cessation of feelings and perceptions".-This is sometimes called the "ninth *jhāna*" in commentarial and scholarly literature.

from ***Dhyāna in Buddhism***
http://en.wikipedia.org/wiki/Dhyana_in_Buddhism

The Ninth Jhana: Cessation

When you reach the limits of perception, you realize that lesser mental activity is better for your calm and peaceful state. You enter a state of "cessation" of consciousness where there is only a very subtle form of perception. The meditator may appear to be unconscious. There have been reports of meditators having heart beats as low as 20 to 40 beats per minute at this jhanic level. The nearest way to describe this state is something like a very deep sleep. The eight and ninth jhanas are not full enlightenment, but very close stepping stones to full awakening. Only those who are very close to being fully enlightened can enter the eighth and especially, the ninth jhana.

9 Jhanas
from ***The Dhamma Encyclopedia***
http://www.dhammawiki.com

58

'Be still, and know that I am God.'

Psalms 46:10

'But seek ye first the kingdom of heaven of God and all these things will be added unto you.'

Matthew 6:33

'.. the kingdom of God is within you.'

Luke 17:21

Holy Bible

Lao Tzu

致虛極
守靜篤

*Zhì xū jí
shǒu jìng dǔ*

**'Empty yourself of everything.
Let the mind rest at peace.'** v16

(translation by Gia-fu Feng and Jane English)

Tao Te Ching of Lao Tzu
c. 6th century BC

Hui Neng
Chinese Ch'an (Zen) Buddhist

Wu-Nien. Zen Buddhists apply this term (meaning literally "no-thought") to meditation on one's own self-nature. Wu-nien does not imply the exclusion of mental activity except in this special kind of meditation. Only when one has achieved the realization of one's own self-nature can one know the essential nature of other minds and other things. Wu-nien is not a cessation of consciousness but, rather, a seeing and a knowing that exclude all attachment and so is called "thoughtlessness" (*wu-nien*). It is related to *shūnyatā* (emptiness): the selfnature cannot be what anything else is. "I am what I am."

Dictionary of Religion and Philosophy,
New York: Paragon House, 1989

Zazen

'When no thought arises in the mind it is called za (sitting) **and to look at one's own nature inwardly is called zen** (meditation).**'**

wu nien

[about *zen* (meditation) & *wu nien* (no thought)]
'Have your mind like unto space and yet entertain in it no thought of emptiness.'

Platform Sutra of Hui-Neng (638-713)

Dazhu HuiHai, 'the Great Pearl'
Chinese Ch'an Buddhist

*'Question: **A little while ago you spoke of refraining from thinking (nien), but you did not finish your explanation.***

*Answer: **It means not fixing your mind upon anything any-where, but totally withdrawing it from the phenomena surrounding you, so that even the thought (szu) of seeking for something does not remain; it means that your mind, confronted by all the forms composing your environment, remains placid and motionless. This abstaining from all thought whatever is called real thought...'** IA 36.1*

Dazhu HuiHai
Zen Teaching of Instantaneous Awakening
9th century

Do-gen Zenji
Japanese Zen Buddhist

'Think the unthinkable.
How to think the unthinkable?
Be without thoughts - this is the
secret of meditation.'

Fukan Zazen-Gi of Do-gen Zenji
13th century

Tilopa
Indian Tantric

'mi-mno - **Don't recall**,
mi-bsam - **Don't imagine**,
mi-shes / mi-sems - **Don't think**,
mi-dpyod - **Don't examine**,
mi-sgom - **Don't control**,
rang-sar-bzhag - **Gather oneself anew.'**

Tilopa (988-1069)

Shri Valmiki Maharshi

'.. by self-effort and self-knowledge make the mind no-mind. Let the infinite consciousness swallow, as it were, the finite mind and then go beyond everything. With your intelligence united with the supreme, hold on to the self which is imperishable.' YV 3.111

'If you give up all thoughts you will here and now attain to the realisation of oneness with all.' YV 3.17

(trans. Venkatesananda - SUNY, 1993)

Yoga Vasistha Maharamayana **of Valmiki**

प्रनष्टश्वासनिश्वासः प्रध्वस्तविषयग्रहः।

निश्चेष्टो निर्विकारश्च लयो जयति योगिनाम्।। ३१।।

उच्छिन्नसर्वसंकल्पो निःशेषाशेषचेष्टितः।

स्वावगम्यो लयः कोऽपि जायते वाग।गोचरः।। ३२।।

लयो लय इति प्राहुः कीदृशं लयलक्षणम्।

अपुनर्वसनोत्थानाल्लयो विषयविस्मृतिः।। ३३।।

pranaṣṭaśvāsaniśvāsaḥ pradhvastaviṣayagrahaḥ |
niśceṣto nirvikāraśca layo jayati yoginām || 31 ||

ucchinnasarvasaṅkalpo niḥśeṣāśeṣaceṣṭitaḥ |
svāvagamyo layaḥ ko'pi jāyate vāga|gocaraḥ || 32 ||

layo laya iti prāhuḥ kīdṛśaṁ layalakśaṇam|
apunarvasanotthānāllayo viṣayavismṛtiḥ || 33 ||

'.. when the mind becomes devoid of all the activities, and remains changeless, then the "yogi" attains to the "laya" stage. ' 4-31

'When all the thoughts and activities are destroyed, then the "laya" stage is produced to describe which is beyond the power of speech, being known by self-experience alone. ' 4-32

'They often speak of "laya", "laya"; but what is meant by "laya"? "laya" is simply the forgetting of the objects of senses when the "vasanas" (desires) do not rise into existence again' 4-33
(trans, Pancham Sinh)

The Hatha Yoga Pradipika
oldest known text on Hatha Yoga exercise c. 14th Century

**Swami Swami Brahmanand Saraswati
Shankaracharya of Jyotir Math**

'According to Upasana Khand of the Vedas we are told:- "yoga" is stopping the fluctuations of consciousness ['yogash-chitta-vritti-nirodhah' - *Yogadarshanam* 1:2].
The ultimate aim is this, that by the practice of having stopped the fluctuations of the inner self, to experience the Supreme form of the Self. Calm without a ripple in any part of the pool of water, that manner a person can see his own face. That really is the method, stopping the fluctuations of the consciousness is really giving a clear reflection of the imperishable self in the instrument of inner vision. This indeed is "darshan" (sight) of the "atma" (self or soul).'

Shri Shankaracharya Vaaksudhaa, p86,
(published 1947)

Shankaracharya Swami Brahmanand Saraswati (1871-1953)

Ramana Maharshi

'In samadhi, there is only the feeling 'I am' and no thoughts. The experience 'I am' is being still'

Maharshi's Gospel, Book 1 - VI - Self-Realisation
http://benegal.org/ramana_maharshi/books/mg/mg006.html

'This 'I'-thought is not pure. It is contaminated with the association of the body and senses. See to whom the trouble is. It is to the 'I'-thought. Hold it. Then the other thoughts vanish.'

Be As You Are: The Teachings of Sri Ramana Maharshi
by David Godman
http://bhagavan-ramana.org/selfenquirymisconceptions.html

'When these thoughts are dispelled, you remain in the state of meditation (aware of awareness), free from thoughts. When the practise becomes firm, your real nature (awareness of awareness) shows itself as true meditation.'

The Self
http://www.theself.com/sri_ramana.cfm

'The limited and multifarious thoughts having disappeared, there shines in the Heart a kind of wordless illumination of 'I - I' which is pure consciousness (Being-ness).'

The Self
http://www.theself.com/sri_ramana.cfm

'What is meditation? It is the suspension of thoughts.'

Simple and Powerful Meditation
http://www.healthmantra.com/bhagwan.shtml

'There are no impediments to meditation. The very thought of such obstacles is the greatest impediment.'

Ramana Maharshi Biography
http://www.energyenhancement.org/
Ramana-Maharshi-Biography-Vichara-Meditation.htm '

Ramana Maharshi (1879-1950)

Swami Sivananda
Founder of Divine Life Society

'Raja Yoga is the king of Yogas. It concerns directly with the mind. In this Yoga there is no struggling with Prana or physical body. There are no Hatha Yogic Kriyas. The Yogi sits at ease, watches his mind and silences the bubbling thoughts. He stills the mind, restrains the thought-waves and enters into the thoughtless state or Asamprajnata Samadhi, Hence the name Raja Yoga.'

from Introduction to **Raja Yoga**, 1937

'ASAMPRAJNATA: Highest superconscious state where the mind is completely annihilated and Reality experienced.'

from Glossary to **Raja Yoga**, 1937

Swami Sivananda Saraswati (1887-1963)

Mahsati Ganjavi
Sufi from Azerbaijan

*'When I went beyond myself,
the pathway finally opened.'*

Mahsati Ganjavi
12th century

Paramahansa Yogananda
Founder of Self-Realisation Fellowship

'In meditation, try to go beyond thinking. As long as thoughts enter the mind, you are functioning on the conscious level.'

A disciple was having difficulty with his meditations. He asked Sri Yogananda, "Am I not trying hard enough?"

'You are trying too hard. You are using too much will power. It becomes nervous.

*Just be relaxed and natural.
As long as you try to meditate, you won't
be able to, just as you can't sleep so long
as you will yourself to sleep. Will power
should be used gradually. Otherwise, it
may become detrimental. That's why it is
better, in the beginning, to emphasize
relaxation.'*

*'Don't feel badly if you find yourself too
restless to meditate deeply. Calmness will
come in time, if you practice regularly.
Just never accept the thought that
meditation is not for you. Remember,
calmness is your eternal, true nature.'*

'Where motion ceases, God begins.'

'Go Deeper Into Meditation'
from ***The Essence of Self-Realisation***
http://www.ananda.org/meditation/free-meditation-
support/articles/paramhansa-yogananda-quotes/

Paramahansa Yogananda (1893-1952)

J Krishnamurti

'Method involves time, does it not? If not now, then eventually, - tomorrow, in a couple of years, - I shall be tranquil. Which means, you do not see the necessity of being tranquil. And so, the "how" becomes a distraction; the method becomes a way of postponing the essentiality of tranquility. And that is why you have all these meditations, these phoney, false controls to get eventual tranquility of the mind, and the various methods of how to discipline in order to acquire that tranquility. Which means you do not see the necessity, the immediate necessity, of having a still mind. When you see the necessity of it, then there is no inquiry into the method at all. Then you see the importance of having a quiet mind, and you have a quiet mind.'

Talk in London, England - 7th April 1952

http://www.holybooks.com/wp-content/uploads/The-Origin-Of-Conflict.pdf

Jiddu Krishnamurti (1895-1986)

Alan Watts

*'The practice of meditation is not what is
ordinarily meant by practice, in the sense of
repetitious preparation for some future
performance. It may seem odd and illogical
to say that meditation, in the form of yoga,
Dhyana, or Za-zen, as used by Hindus and
Buddhists, is a practice without purpose – in
some future time – because it is the art of
being completely centered in the here and
now.'*

'Meditation is therefore the art of suspending verbal and symbolic thinking for a time, somewhat as a courteous audience will stop talking when a concert is about to begin.

Simply sit down, close your eyes, and listen to all sounds that may be going on – without trying to name or identify them. Listen as you would listen to music. If you find that verbal thinking will not drop away, don't attempt to stop it by force of will-power. Just keep your tongue relaxed, floating easily in the lower jaw, and listen to your thoughts as if they were birds chattering outside – mere noise in the skull – and they will eventually subside of themselves, as a turbulent and muddy pool will become calm and clear if left alone.'

'The Practice of Meditation'
from ***Way of Liberation*** pp91-95

Alan Watts (1915-1973)

Maharishi Mahesh Yogi
'Transcendental Meditation' - 'TM'

'Those who meditate, they retire from the outside, they take their awareness from the outside and gradually go deep into the thinking process and eventually go beyond the thought. Transcend thought and then the thinking mind, the conscious mind becomes consciousness. When it goes beyond thought then it transcends thought and becomes consciousness. This consciousness is pure consciousness. The nature of this pure consciousness is bliss. It is non-changing sphere of life because we have transcended all the variable section of relative life and gone to the Absolute. This is called Being, Inner Being, Absolute Bliss consciousness.'

Seven States of Consciousness
- recorded lecture USA - 1967

'As long as the thinking mind is experiencing a thought, so long the mind is a thinker and the thought becomes finer and finer, then the thinker becomes more and more alert in order to experience the finer thought, and then the thought becomes finer and finer, it becomes finest and when the thought drops off, the thinker remains all by himself and this is self-realization.
What I have to do to realize myself? I have only to stop realizing things from within and see that I don't go to sleep.'

Seven States of Consciousness
- recorded lecture USA - 1967

Maharishi Mahesh Yogi (1918-2008)

Acharya Rajneesh
Bhagwan
Osho
Dynamic Meditation

'Really, there can be no method as far as meditation is concerned. Meditation is not a method. Through technique, through method, you cannot go beyond mind. When you leave all methods, all techniques, you transcend mind.'

Lecture at the invitation of Maharishi Mahesh Yogi, with questions & answers, Pahalgam, Kashmir 1969
http://o-meditation.com/osho/osho-meets-with-followers-of-maharishi-mahesh-yogi/

Acharya Rajneesh (1931-90)

'When you are not doing anything at all, bodily, mentally... on no level, then all activity has ceased, and you simply are, just to be.... That's what meditation is.'

'Meditation is a Very Simple Phenomenon' video
http://www.youtube.com/watch?v=0peVQTdI3Yg

Osho (1931-1990)

Mataji Nirmala Devi
Sahaja Yoga

'In meditation you have to be absolutely effortless, expose yourself fully and you have to be absolutely thoughtless at that time.

If you are not thoughtless, at that time you have to just watch your thoughts, but do not get involved into them. You will find gradually, as when the sun rises, darkness goes away and the sun's rays go into every part and make the whole place enlightened. In the same way, your being will be completely enlightened. But if you put in an effort at that time or try to stop something within you, it will not happen. Effortlessness is the only way into meditation, but you should not be lethargic about it. You should be alert and watch it.'

'Effortless Meditation' - London, 1st January 1980
http://shrimataji.org/site/in-her-words/shri-mataji-reading-room/
effortless-meditation.html

Shri Mataji Nirmala Devi (1923-2011)

Nisargadatta Maharaj

'To remain without thought in the waking state is the greatest worship.'

I Am (Existence, Consciousness)

http://www.theself.com/sri_nisargadatta.cfm

'As long as you are a beginner certain formalised meditations, or prayers may be good for you. But for a seeker for reality there is only one meditation - the rigorous refusal to harbour thoughts. To be free from thoughts is itself meditation....You begin by letting thoughts flow and watching them.

The very observation slows down the mind till it stops altogether. Once the mind is quiet, keep it quiet. Don't get bored with peace, be in it, go deeper into it....Watch your thoughts and watch yourself watching the thoughts. The state of freedom from all thoughts will happen suddenly and by the bliss of it you shall recognise it. '

(translation by Maurice Frydman)

I Am That p.224f

'When thus the mind becomes completely silent, it shines with a new light and vibrates with new knowledge. It all comes spontaneously, you need only hold on to the 'I am' '

(translation by Maurice Frydman)

I Am That p.332

Nisargadatta Maharaj (1897- 1981)

contemplatio - prayer not using thoughts or emotions.

"Contentless meditation" doesn't use emotions or thoughts - not even spiritual thoughts. It's often called simply meditation or thought-free meditation. It does not develop thoughts, images, or feelings, but rather rests attentively, receptively, in awareness, in the presence of God, with the intention of consenting to the presence and action of God in oneself. You do this without identifying with any thoughts or feelings that may spontaneously arise.

You don't reject, suppress or block the thoughts, by the way - you just let go of them, without the affirmation "this is I" or "this is my thought". And you rest attentively and receptively in the space between each thought and the next. Those spaces may grow a little, though new thoughts will probably keep coming. One reason for avoiding the use of even spiritual thoughts during contemplative prayer is that at this time you intend to be present to God, not to an idea or image of God. Actually, it's not so much a matter of avoidance but rather not-identifying-oneself-with the thoughts. Another reason is that the ordinary self, which is maintained by thoughts and emotions and by identification with them, is to be given a rest during these practices. And just think of all that "surrendering" training you get by not hanging on to each thought.'

Christian Contemplative Practice
http://www.easterspirit.com/ContemplativePractices.htm

Carmelite Sisters
Most Sacred Heart of Los Angeles

'.. in meditation the method used is intended to lead to a prayer beyond all methods, that is contemplative prayer. Contemplation is often a misunderstood word. It is not a prayer that we can initiate or cause to happen. It is divinely produced and no amount of action on our part can produce or prolong it.'

'We have entered into a wordless prayer, an awareness of the Divine Guest within, not through the use of the intellect but through a knowing loving, a deep communion with the Triune God. It is a prayer of quiet calmness in which we drink deeply at the life-giving fount.'

from ***Meditation and Contemplation…
What's the Difference?***
http://www.integratedcatholiclife.org/2013/07/ask-a-carmelite-
difference-between-meditation-and-contemplation/'

Carmelite Sisters

Bhante G
Theravada Buddhist monk
Founder Bhavana Society

'Once your mind is free from thought, it becomes clearly wakeful and at rest in an utterly simple awareness. This awareness cannot be described adequately.'

Mindfulness in Plain English
Chapter 16, p171
http://www.vipassana.com/meditation/
mindfulness_in_plain_english_18.php

Bhante Henepola Gunaratana b.1927

Chokyi Nyima Rinpoche
Tibetan Buddhist lama

'Meditation training, in the sense of sustaining the nature of mind, is a way of being free from clinging and the conceptual attitude of forming thoughts, and therefore free from the causes of samsara: karma and disturbing emotions. Please do not believe that liberation and samsara is somewhere over there: it is here, in oneself. Thought is samsara. Being free of thought is liberation. When we are free of thinking, we are free of thought.'

Thought-Free Wakefulness

http://www.shambhalasun.com/index.php?
option=content&task=view&id=1660

Dzogchen Master Chokyi Nyima Rinpoche
b.1951

Samsara. The cycle of birth and rebirth as understood in Hindu teaching. It is dictated by the karmic principle. (See Karma.) Samsara implies bondage: only by the control of thoughts and desires can human beings overcome that bondage and be liberated in such a way as to transcend the cycle. Karma and Samsara imply both biological and spiritual evolution and a relation between human beings and lower forms of animal life such as imposes on the former the duty of compassion toward the latter: reverence not only for human but for all life.

Geddes MacGregor
Dictionary of Religion and Philosophy,
New York: Paragon House, 1989

Karma. *Sanskrit* term meaning "deed" or "action". The karmic principle is the basic principle of the spiritual dimension of being. It is a principle of balance. Although commonly associated with Hinduism, Buddhism, and other oriental religions, it can be seen as expressive of the Torah in Judaism, considered as the eternal principle of righteousness embodied in the written Torah and also as expressed in the Golden Rule, to be found in Confucius, in Kant's Categorical Imperative, and in the form laid down by Jesus: "Do unto others as ye would have others do unto you." Contrary to the vulgar misunderstanding of it as a fatalistic principle, it is in fact a principle that preeminently implies and is based upon freedom of choice. It is associated with the principle of Reincarnation and may be thought to imply it. Actions, good or bad, have consequences upon the karma of each individual. Each individual has a karmic inheritance, good and bad, and sooner or later must work off the bad and develop the good.

Geddes MacGregor
Dictionary of Religion and Philosophy,
New York: Paragon House, 1989

THE KNACK OF MEDITATION